Mariju

The Ultimate Marijuana Grower Handbook for Cultivation of Heavy Cannabis Harvest Production Including Extract Preparation and Mouthwatering Easy Edible Recipes

Table of Contents

electronically or in print. This extends to creating a secondary or tertiary copy of the work or a recorded copy and is only allowed with the express written consent from the Publisher. All additional right reserved.

The information in the following pages is broadly considered a truthful and accurate account of facts and as such, any inattention, use, or misuse of the information in question by the reader will render any resulting actions solely under their purview. There are no scenarios in which the publisher or the original author of this work can be in any fashion deemed liable for any hardship or damages that may befall them after undertaking information described herein.

Additionally, the information in the following pages is intended only for informational purposes and should thus be thought of as universal. As befitting its nature, it is presented without assurance regarding its prolonged validity or interim quality. Trademarks that are mentioned are done without written consent and can in no way be considered an endorsement from the trademark holder.

Introduction

I am thrilled that you have chosen to learn more about how to grow marijuana. You might be standing by to cultivate a crop of the 'weed,' but you just have not been able to locate a reference manual that clearly states how to grow it. Well, now you will know what to do and what not to do while on your new journey. Many individuals make the process more complicated than it has to be because you can cultivate your budget, growing space, and desired yield amounts whether it is in a backyard garden or hiding in your closed home.

The Marijuana Growing: Ultimate Marijuana Grower Handbook for Cultivation of Heavy Cannabis Harvest Production Including Extract Preparation and Mouthwatering Easy Edibles Recipes will prove how easy the process is just a few minutes daily to maintain your hoard planted outdoors. You can have your own professional stash ready for consumption for whatever reason you have in mind. The main issues can include theft of the plants, privacy, deer or other critters, and the possibility of pollination.

Cannabis has been around and used in medicine for centuries with its three species and seven sub-species. The medieval physicians used the plant to treat many ailments by mixing the plant into teas and other medicines.

During ancient times, hemp was considered a food source. Buds, seeds, flowers, and roots from the cannabis plant have been used as a paste, powder, oil, edibles, drinks, and drugs for thousands of years. Hemp does not have the identical effects as presented by marijuana and is just one of the cannabis plant varieties.

Fast forward to the 1500s when cannabis was brought by the Spanish to South America, but it was not introduced into North America until many years later as a medicinal drug.

BONUS: This book also includes the FREE gift !

Follow this link (https://bit.ly/2RCY57l) and find out, what are the 5 essential tools every grower needs to have in his arsenal, what tools have the highest quality over time and where to get them for the lowest price.

Tip: A bit of caution, if you attempt these methods; be sure it is legal to do so in your area.

Chapter 1: Basic Facts and Terminology

Before you begin growing your own cannabis or making your own extracts, it is essential to understand some basic facts about the plant, how it is used, and basic terminology. This chapter will start with the basic knowledge and vocabulary involved with the growing of marijuana.

The Endocannabinoid System

The human body has a natural endocannabinoid system that is present in the brain, the central nervous system, and the immune system. The cannabinoids bind to receptors in these systems. This system allows the cannabis to affect the body with its various cannabinoid compounds.

There are two types of endocannabinoid receptors found in the body. They are the CB1 and CB2 receptors. Different cannabinoid compounds interact with the receptors differently. Hence, some cannabinoids cause different effects in the receptors.

Cannabinoids

Cannabinoids are cannabis compounds that are found within the marijuana plant. There is a wide range of cannabinoids in the marijuana plant, and some of those compounds are psychoactive. There are over 100 identified cannabinoids in the cannabis plant. These cannabinoids bind to the receptors naturally found in the human body. The receptors are part of the endocannabinoid system that delivers the cannabinoids and bonds them to receptors throughout the body. Two of the significant cannabinoids are THC and CBD:

- THC, also known as tetrahydrocannabinol, is the primary psychoactive cannabinoid in the marijuana plant. It is this compound that gets a marijuana user high. The higher the percentage of THC in the bud,
the more powerful the high is. The various strains

of marijuana have different strengths.

The strength also differs in the different ways of consuming it. There are several ways of consuming cannabis such as smoking, vaping, eating or drinking it. The user feels high when THC bonds to endocannabinoid receptors in the brain. The bonding of the compound and the receptors is what produces the psychoactive effect in the user, such as getting high.

- CBD, also known as cannabidiol, is another type of cannabinoid, but it is non-psychoactive, which means that CBD does not cause the user to feel high. Because CBD is non-psychoactive, it is often used for medical marijuana. Therefore, it retains many of the plant's benefits without having the psychoactive effects. CBD comes in mouth drops, oils, lotions, and CBD infused edibles.

- As of the time of this writing, CBD is legal federally, but the various states need to choose if they will legalize it. CBD is now available in most states; even many that don't have medical marijuana.

Medical Benefits

Both THC and CBD have a multitude of medical benefits. Studies show that cannabinoids can treat a wide range of diseases from multiple sclerosis, anxiety disorders, PTSD, seizures, and other health benefits. In many cases, either CBD or THC can help with the medical issue. Due to this, many states have legalized medical marijuana.

Terminology

Below is a list of vocabulary listing of the language used throughout the marijuana culture and terms specifically for growing the marijuana plant.

- **Cannabis**: The technical name for the marijuana plant and the products derived from it.

- **Marijuana**: The most commonly used name for cannabis and the cannabis plant is marijuana.
- **Bud**: A slang term for the plant material of the marijuana plant. It refers to the bud of the flower.
- **Pot**: A slang term for cannabis.
- **Weed**: A slang term for cannabis. This often refers specifically to the plant matter of the cannabis plant.
- **Edible**: A food or drink that is infused with marijuana and is ingested rather than smoked or vaped.
- **Extract**: An extract is a form of cannabis that has been transformed from plant matter into a resin form. Extracts have more potency than smoking or vaping plant matter.
- **Smoking**: Smoking is when you burn the plant matter, specifically the bud of the plant, and inhale the smoke. Examples of smoking marijuana include smoking the substance out of pipes or bongs.

- **Vaping**: Vaping is a process where the plant matter is heated up until it turns into a vapor, which is then inhaled. Examples of vapes include hand-held models like pens and desktop machines which are more fixed and stabilized. Some desktop models include a balloon or whip that you fill with vapor and then inhale from.

- **Dabbing**: Dabbing is the process of turning the extract into vapor and inhaling it. Dabbing is done by heating up a nail or a bucket in a rig and placing the extract on that hot surface to vaporize it. Alternately, the extract can be placed in a small dish. A nectar collector is then heated up and touches the extract in the plate. This produces vapor. Most people use a butane torch to heat their rig or nectar collector.

- **Wax**: A type of extract. It is referred to as wax since the extract is in a soft resin form that appears wax-like.

- **A Shatter**: A type of extract that is unlike wax, shatter is a solid and to dab it, you break off small pieces to place in the rig or in the dish.
- **Cannabis Oil**: Cannabis is an oil form that can be used in cooking or rubbed into the skin for use as an anti-inflammatory medication.
- **Cannabis Butter**: Cannabis butter, also called canna-butter or hash butter, is butter that is infused with cannabis and used for cooking.
- **Cannabinoid**: Cannabinoids are chemical compounds found in the cannabis plant. These compounds include THC, CDB, and many other cannabinoids. Scientists have identified over 100 cannabinoids.
- **Indica**: One of the two major types of cannabis plants. Indica tends to have a calm high that leads to deep relaxation.
- **Sativa**: One of the two major types of cannabis plants. Sativa tends to have an energetic high.

- **Ruderalis**: A type of cannabis plant. Ruderalis is a low-THC variety of cannabis plant. Ruderalis is rarely grown.

- **Organic Marijuana**: Marijuana that is grown without the use of pesticides or other commercial chemicals.

- **Medium**: The medium is a substance used in growing plants. The most common medium is soil, but some advanced growers use Rockwool cubes.

- **pH**: pH is a 14-point scale that measures the acidity of the medium that the marijuana plant is grown in.

- **Carbon Dioxide**: Carbon dioxide, also known as CO_2 is a gas that plants use in photosynthesis. Plants use CO_2 in a manner similar to humans breathing oxygen.

- **Nutrient**: The chemical elements and compounds that a plant needs to grow. These elements include nitrogen, calcium, magnesium, potassium, phosphorus, sulfur, oxygen, carbon, and hydrogen.

- **Indoor Growing**: Growing marijuana in an indoor environment is accomplished in a room in your house or a greenhouse.

- **Outdoor Growing**: Growing marijuana in an outdoor environment includes areas such as in a garden or in pots on the porch.

- **Hydroponic**: A way of indoor growing that uses water filtration systems.

- **Cabinet**: Cabinets are pre-built rectangular boxes with built-in lighting, ventilation, and pots for growing in. Cabinets are typically used by advanced growers.

- **Clone**: A genetic duplicate of the mother plant. Clones are created from taking cuttings off of another plant and then planting it.

- **Sea of Green**: A Sea of Green (SOG) grow is an indoor grow where the grower uses lighting to force the plants to flower earlier than usual.

- **The Screen of Green**: A Screen of Green (ScrOG) grow is a type of indoor grow unit where the grower uses a filter screen to increase the number of buds getting light.

- **Germination**: Germination is the process of growing plants from seeds. Germination is the first stage in the plants' life cycle. Germination is often started with seeds in cheesecloth or wet paper towels.
- **Flower**: The flower of the marijuana plant.
- **Harvest**: Harvesting is when the buds are collected from the plants.
- **Drying**: The process of drying out the buds to prepare them for consumption of the plant.
- **Grow Lights**: Special lights that are used to grow plants indoors.
- **Propagation Kits**: Propagation kits are starter kits that can raise many seeds in the early germination state of the plants' life cycle.

Chapter 2: The Marijuana Plant

Like basic concepts and terminology, you need to have an understanding of the marijuana plant itself. This chapter will cover the plant in regard to sex as well as other characteristics.

The Marijuana Plant

The cannabis or marijuana plant is a type of plant that produces cannabinoids. It is famous for its five leaves that spread out in a fan-like fashion, but it can also have seven or nine leaves. The marijuana plant isn't just used for cannabinoids, it is also used for recreational or medicinal purposes and for industrial uses. The marijuana plant is also grown for hemp fiber, an industrial material that can be used in many industries, specifically textiles. Hemp makes very strong and stable fibers when turned into cloth.

The marijuana plant can grow virtually in any

environment. It is a very rugged plant that lives in resilient places and also thrives when grown in indoor growing systems. The marijuana plant is cultivated worldwide in many varied environments.

Sex of Plants

There are several sexes of plants. There are male and female plants, just like human gender, but there are also hermaphrodite and sinsemilla plants. The favored sex for marijuana growing is the female plant. The female plant produces the most THC and has the best medicinal effects.

Male plants pollinate the female plant, allowing it to reproduce. Male plants are suitable for genetics as they will pass on traits like mold resistance to their offspring. However, many growers choose to clone their female plants instead of using male plants to pollinate and reproduce since this ensures that the grower has all female plants.

Hermaphrodite plants are both male and female,

and they can pollinate/fertilize themselves.

Sinsemilla plants have an unusually high amount of psychoactive cannabinoids, making them sought after by growers.

Anatomy of the Plant

There is more to the marijuana plant than just the bud. There are several structures on the plant, and it is essential to understand the anatomy of the plant before starting to grow. Below are the compositions of the marijuana plant:

- **Colas**: The cola is the location on the plant where the buds come together at the stem. The cola only appears on the female plant. The cola size and quantity are increased by trimming or trimming the plant.
- **Calyx**: The calyx is the actual bud or first part of the cannabis flower formation. Its little green leaves are called sepals which overlap the formed bud where the flower develops to act as a protective covering of the flower.

- **Trichomes**: The Greek meaning of trichome is trikoma which means hair. These trichomes are essentially the resin glands which secrete the THC; appearing as liquid globules to make the bud sticky. As they mature, the colors go from clear, to white, to a dusky orange with a final shade of reddish brown. The more mature the flower is at harvest, the more balanced in potency it will be. Recall, at harvest time the trichomes are what produce the resin.

- **Pistil**: The components of the pistil or the reproductive female organ of the flower are the ovary, style, and stigma. The pistils are the 'hairs' that emerge from the calyx.

- **Plant Nodes**: The launch pad for leaves and stems are found on the stalk (the nodes). The internodal spacing is the distance between one node and the next. They are where the little 'V' branches form the stalk.

- **Sugar Leaves**: The small leaves clustered around the buds are dusted with what looks like sugar crystals. This is the tetrahydrocannabinol (THC) which is used to make hash or edibles.

- **Fan Leaves**: These leaves are the largest on the plant and capture light like a solar panel. They also provide shade for the plant on sunny days.

Indica vs Sativa

As mentioned, there are two main strains of marijuana. They are Indica and Sativa. The two sub-species each have their own medicinal and psychoactive properties.

Indica is known for having the following medical benefits:

- Muscle relaxation
- Increased mental relaxation
- Decreased acute pain
- Decreased nausea

- Increased appetite

Sativa is known for having the following medical benefits:

- Anti-depressant
- Anti-anxiety
- Increased focus and creativity
- Reduced chronic pain

Chapter 3: Growing Techniques

Cannabis plants are generally adaptable but are very susceptible to extreme weather conditions. Temperatures about 86°F/30°C will cause the plants to stop growing, but below 55°F/13°C can stunt the growth pattern, and possibly kill the plant.

If you live where temperatures rise above 86°F/30°C, try locating a spot where you can receive some filtered sun during the hottest times of the day. If you are in an extremely hot area, choose an area that has a constant breeze, but will also include a space that will provide more water as needed.

For the colder climates, try planting in areas that retain heat such as a south-facing fence or brick wall; whereas those in the hotter climates should avoid this element.

High winds or heavy rains can also cause reduced yields as well as physical damage, including powdery mildew or mold, especially during its flowering stage. Consider planting near some type of windbreakers such as a large shrub, fence, or wall.

The lengths of the days also have an effect on the plant's growth. You can reference climate zone map to discover multiple elements including the proximity of large bodies of water and elevation to assist you with your growing plants. If you know any local veggie or flower growers, he/she will be an excellent reference point for your area.

Climate and THC

Many elements are involved when you consider growing your cannabis outdoors. Maybe you have decided to produce a plant with a high content of THC, but you need to contemplate that the high cannabidiol (CBD) plants perform best if planted in a warm climate. This is the scoop on that pattern.

The CBD plants are the runner-up to THC when it comes to its average volume. The CBD creates anti-anxiety, anti-inflammatory, and analgesic properties without the 'stoned' or 'high' psychoactive effects provided by THC. However, THC is the most active compound, but you have to consider that there are at least 85 other compounds.

Effects of Latitude

Lower latitudes, such as San Diego with early season varieties, will have flowering induced early in the season even during the maturing process and will remain small. The higher latitudes such as Boston will usually have shorter nights during the summer which provide more of a chance for the plant to develop into mature buds. In other words, it won't trigger during the early part of the summer in lower latitudes, but it will flower earlier because of the milder climate and more extended nighttime hours.

Many varieties and flowering habits have led to many different growing strategies. Areas which stay warm year around, sativa-indica varieties and sativas can be planted in the fall. They will grow throughout the winter as the flower and become ready 70 to 80 days after they have been planted.

Where to Plant with the Correct Lighting

If you decide to plant outside, the sun will provide your plants with approximately eight hours daily—under ideal situations. Your plants need a minimum of five to six hours of direct lighting daily to remain healthy. The most beneficial hours are from 10 in the morning until 4 in the afternoon when the direct lighting source is stronger.

Consult the Internet for local people and maps for locating sun-facing locations. You can also use the method used for centuries. The sun always "rises in the east and sets in the west." At noon, the sun is directly over your head. Take advantage of prechecking the location before you plant using the 10 a.m. to 4 p.m. timeline.

You will need to shield your crop from strong wind gusts by planting around thick bushes or a small earth bank. These methods can also dissuade any invasion from unwelcome animals and humans wanting a few of your greens.

Choose a location with a good water source such as by a lake or stream. The crop needs to be accessible to a water supply during the hot summer months.

When to Plant

If you live in the northern hemisphere, growing schedules are usually from the end of April or the first part of May until October. It is a common practice to begin the germination of seeds indoors for a headstart on the growing season. You can use lights indoors for a few weeks until the season is ready for you to plant. Gradually put the plants outside during the daylight hours until they are sturdy enough to be placed in a permanent spot.

You can also begin the process outdoors in early April in a greenhouse or under a piece of glass. If you are lucky and have a Mediterranean type climate, you can use your private terrace for a secluded spot for your plants.

Expected Yields

The female plant can yield between 100–400 grams depending on the strain, as well as the nutrition provided, sowing time, and sunlight factors.

If you use a space where you can plant the weed three to five feet apart—under perfect conditions, you can expect to yield approximately 17.5 ounces or 500 grams of marijuana for each plant. To provide the plants time to grow large, you should germinate the seeds early (more on that in later chapters).

The Growing Medium and Friendly Nutrients

Cannabis requires slightly acidic soil with organic matter in a well-drained space.

To grow a healthy cannabis plant, you have to start with the right growing medium. You can choose from soilless mixes, soil, hydroponics, and other ways.

- **Soil**: You can begin with a mix called Fox Farms Ocean Forest soil. You want to grow the cannabis in a composted organic soil. The soil is comprised of three primary constituents including silt, sand, and clay.
- **No Soil**: Hydroponic growing is anything but soil, such as perlite, coco coir, and vermiculite.
- **Hydroponics/Direct into the Water**: Some of the most significant yields and fastest growth use this method.

You should think about composting your own soil versus purchasing pre-packaged soil which is more expensive. However, you need to consider that the pre-packaged products have been supplemented with nutrients that will boost your new plant growth. If you compost, it's free, but you will need to add excellent cannabis nutrients. Some of the professionals use regular/organic potting mixes with the exception of one product.

Heavy clay soils do not hold oxygen and drain slowly and will require some amendments. About one month before planting is to begin, dig large holes on the site where you intend to plant your crop. Combine peat moss, compost, and coco coir to help bind the soil, while at the same the mixture provides air for circulation and food. If you are in a hot climate, sandy soil will help keep the plants cooler, and the water retention will also be beneficial.

Check lake bottoms and older riverbeds for the best silty loam to use as a growing medium. It warms quickly, is easy to work, and holds moisture. The silty content also contains many essential nutrients, as well as providing proper drainage for the plants. If you can locate an area with this crumbly dark soil, you won't need to make any additions to its contents.

Some growers believe that it is okay to use the same type of soil you would use to grow corn and tomatoes, so you could always pretend that you are a 'farmer' and want to inquire about which product the company provides.

A Soil Test Kit

In essence, there isn't a 'perfect' soil solution for good performance, but it is good to know the type of soil. You need to consider pH and factors including loam and clay content or sand content of the soil. You can purchase a testing kit from most garden centers. Your pH factor should be between the limits of 5.8 and 6.5 with sufficient nutrients and good drainage as additional features.

If you would rather have fewer headaches, it is reasonably inexpensive to have your soil tested to discover the pH factors. A testing agency will notify you of any contaminants in the soil sample and will recommend specific fertilizers or other materials to amend the soil content.

Chapter 4: Advanced Growing Techniques

Achieve More Than One Harvest

More than one harvest can be done in some areas such as Hawaii, southern parts of North America, and Australia because of the light provided throughout the entire year.

Some growers believe that it is possible to purchase auto-flowering marijuana seeds since they will grow from seeds to harvest in ten weeks. If you live in a temperate climate, it is possible to have two harvests in one season. This is the scoop:

- Once most of the crop is removed, leave most of the leaves and the tiny buds.
- Simply, begin the process right away that led to the first growth cycle.
- Add some fresh fertilizer and lots of water to re-stimulate another growth spurt.

By removing the leaves, you are providing the activation because that is what absorbs the sunlight which the plants need for energy regrowth. Since the sunlight intensity and timing has already changed, the flowers are already in the flowering stage.

Another hint if you are in a tropical climate with mild temperatures through fall, your plants can vegetate longer. You can use manipulation with a light source such as leaving a flashlight on the plants during the nighttime/dark phase.

If you are fruitful with the period of darkness, you will have the flowering stage rebooted. Once they begin the second flowering stage, stop the light interruption.

For example, if you expect colder weather or frost that will arrive within two weeks, you should begin the flowering process three weeks before that time.

The Nutrients You Should Use

The nutrient setup can become confusing for first-time growers because each one will create different products for different purposes. Each stage of the plant's life requires a different one. You must know the correct nitrogen, phosphorous, and potassium levels. If you are curious why the 'K' is in there, it is because the name is derived from Neo-Latin which is kalium. If you want to search for a fertilizer with ratios of the NPK of a 5:1:5 ratio process easier, this is a calculation of nutrient ratios:

NPK Values for Growing Cannabis			
Plant Stage	N	P	K
Vegetative	High	Medium	High
Flowering	Low	Medium to high	High

If you purchase a high-quality soil for the vegetative stage, the plants will use the soil's nutrients for the first three or four weeks, so you can skip adding the additional nutrients.

Start the vegetative nutrients when the first leaves open. As you see, for the low-nitrogen formula, use Bloom with loads of 'P' and 'K' for the flowering stage which is essential during the budding developmental stage.

The potassium will motivate the weight/bulk of the flowers, and the phosphorous will increase the flower count. Use caution and don't over-do it because you will burn the plants.

Nitrogen and the Flowering Stage

Bud development is downcast if the nitrogen content is high during the flowering stage, as well as leaving a nasty taste on the buds; the fundamental reason why you should not use a general-purpose plant nutrient during this phase of the plant's development.

Substitute: In desperation; use succulents or cactus plant food during this phase until you can provide better nutrients since they have high levels of 'P' and 'K' but low quantities of 'N.'

Test the Water Supply for pH Levels

You must be attentive with the water because the 'weed' cannot absorb the necessary nutrients with a pH that is not within tolerable ranges. A digital pH pen will be your best friend. These are the optimum pH factors:

- Coco coir: 5.5 to 6.5
- Hydroponics: 5.5 to 6.5
- Soil: 6.0 to 7.0

Choices for Potting Mixes in the United States

Many of the professional cannabis growers believe that *Miracle-Gro Potting Mix* is not good for growing cannabis because it contains nitrogen which is slowly released. Nitrogen is excellent for vegetable growing; but during the flowering stage with the bud growth, you will not be able to rinse the nitrogen out. You will have a product that has a chemical taste, as well as the possibility of lower yields of your pot. It is also known for poor drainage which could further damage your plants. Also, never use fertilizer spikes which also contain the slow-released nitrogen.

If you want to use Miracle-Gro, choose the Organic Choice Potting Mix since it does not contain the slow-release nutrients which are a much better choice than the original version. Conversely, it may still have poor drainage even with the use of perlite; but, it is possible that you still want to use the product.

Other organic fertilizers can include blood meal, bat guano, worm castings, bone meal, and similar ingredients to improve the condition of the soil before your seeds are ready for planting. The compost should be prepared early as well.

Perlite and Coco Coir

Purchasing a bag of perlite will help the soil to drain better. You need to mix 30% perlite to 70% soil. The perlite looks like white rocks before it is mixed. Mixing coco coir with the perlite is a good start for the medium since it is easily maintained.

The coco coir holds the water, inexpensive, and doesn't have issues such as root problems and bugs which are commonly associated with soil.

Chemical vs Organic Nutrients

Each of these choices is beneficial for different reasons. It will depend on the following elements:

Chemicals

- Faster growth
- Increased potency
- Hydro's only choice

Organic

- More natural

- Better taste and smell of the buds
- Not usable for hydro

Grow and Bloom Fertilizer

You will need to switch to a bloom fertilizer during the flowering stage. During the first and the second week, grow fertilizer is used because the plant needs the extra nutrients as a building block to reproduce as well as become taller. You can control the size of the plant by managing the fertilizer. If you have limited space or just want to keep the plant smaller, start giving the plant bloom fertilizer. You will only observe a couple of centimeters, but it is the product quantity to consider.

Bloom Fertilizer

After approximately three weeks, the maximum size should have been reached and don't need to grow taller. The bloom fertilizer will provide more potassium and phosphorus which are central building blocks to ensure proper bud formation.

PK 13/14 is a good choice; but, always check the bottle for the amount to use. Your plant will let you know what it needs.

Check with some of these types of liquid organic bloom formulas including Fox Farm Big Bloom or Iguana Juice unless you have a preferred brand already in mind.

Foliar Feeding

If your fertilizer is sufficient, you may not need foliar feeding; but, sometimes it is problematic to get the fertilizer 'just right.' If you provide the foliar feeding, the nutrients will be quickly absorbed, so the deficiencies from the lack of fertilizer will be corrected. It is advisable to administer the 'feeding' before the sun becomes too robust. Early in the day is best. It is done this way to reduce the risk of mold. It would be sprayed once or twice weekly on top of the leaves.

Locate the Seeds: Types & Germination

If you are a beginner, this chapter should provide you with some valuable information.

High Times Top Five List

If you have wondered what the best buds are, who would know better than High Times? The top five are shown by the potency through lab testing and location of where the plants were grown. The list is from 2015 from the California area which gives you an idea of the most robust CBD strains with a knockout punch:

- Emperor Cookie Dough—31.1% THC (Hybrid Flowers, US)
- Karma-sutra—29.72% THC (Medical Hybrid)
- Strawberry Banana—28.4 (Medical Hybrid)
- Veganic Strawberry Cough—28.31 (Sativa, US)

- Life is Good OG (bxOGF6)—27.2 (Medical Indica)

The Top Seed Banks

According to *Top Seed Banks*, this list is up-to-date with banks worldwide. The strains have been tested (in most cases) for CBD and THC levels.

- **Greenman's Seed Bank**: Twenty years of life has been dedicated to this bank by Greenman which has indicated the source as a legit bank to purchase your seeds with freight worldwide including Australia and the United States. The industry changes quickly; but, it is an excellent choice for the best Indica, Sativa, Hybrid, Autos, and Feminized seeds. The service provided has been deemed as the safest seed bank of 2016.
- **Amsterdam Marijuana Seeds**: Amsterdam provides a huge seed list of for outdoor planting. The site offers a filter for

the growing difficulties such as "easy, moderate, and expert," so you don't choose a plant which you are not qualified to nurture. The company guarantees delivery with an 8.2 customer rating involving 5323 participants. Worldwide shipping is offered throughout Europe, Australia, Canada, the United States, and other continents.

- **British Columbia Seed Company**: Award-winning strains are offered and have been since Vancouver, Canada opened the doors to the seed company in 1995—making it the oldest seed company still under operation in North America. Over 30,000 satisfied customers were serviced in 2016 with the best seeds for the buck. They will ship globally to any country. The BSCA never uses hermaphrodites—just 'true' females and males make the seed cut. Proper germination is tested periodically. The company boasts over the best annual strain for 2016 as the Pot of Gold. She appears as a bronzed golden plant with so many gold trichomes which was bred by the best Dutch breeder in Amsterdam. Currently, over 100 plants are available for shipment. Reviews from 5323 participants deemed the service rating at 8.2.

- Another bustling location can be found on the site about I Love Growing Marijuana, (https://shop.ilovegrowingmarijuana.com/ collections/outdoor)which also offers many different types of seeds. You can order by categories such as by outdoor/cool, outdoor/sunny by the climate or by the plant type of Sativa dominant or Indica dominant. Germination is guaranteed with free worldwide delivery in a discreetly packaged delivery box.

Types of Seeds and Germination

Cannabis plants have two main classifications; Sativa and auto-flowering which are further explained:

- **Auto-flowering Cannabis Explained**

Improved breeding techniques have discovered an auto-flowering strain that makes it possible to grow high-potency, abundant crops within nine to ten weeks from the germination stage to harvest. It is a descendant from the wild *Cannabis ruderalis* populations located in China, Russia, Eastern Europe, and other locations including northern and central Asia. Some of the botanists classify the species as a subspecies of C. Sativa or C. Indica.

Over the past five years or so, the strains have significantly improved making it a 'hit' in the cannabis community of growers. The *C. ruderalis* reaches a height of about 90 cm (approximately three feet) as a short-statured plant, and tend to transition to the flowering stage after approximately fourteen to twenty-one days after germination. Most of these plants can be harvested in as short of time as six and a half weeks.

These are excellent plants which are resistant to cold temperatures, pests, and diseases. You can also grow them in a low-quality soil without a lot of nutrients.

Some of the common auto-flower strains include these:

- Northern Lights
- Sensi Skunk
- Low Ryder
- Blue Cheese
- White Widow
- Amnesia Haze

- **Sativa Plants Explained**

Sativa's origin revolves from some parts of South America, as well as South East and Central Asia. Carolus Linnaeus, a Swedish botanist, classified the plant in 1753. The plant can give you the 'head-high' but still leaves you with enough energy to complete whatever it is you need to do for the day.

It can lead to a mild case of insomnia if smoked at night because of the 'energetic' elements of the product. If you have these issues, it might be a good idea to search for a Sativa dominant hybrid.

In a single season, it can reach as much as twenty feet with its thin/tall structure. A fruity, sweet flavor is one of its features and can be noticeable in these:

- Amnesia Haze
- Acapulco Gold
- Voodoo Haze
- Liberty Haze
- Purple Haze
- Grey Haze
- Super Silver Haze
- Sour Diesel

Get the High-Quality Seeds

If you want to produce a profitable crop, you need to be sure they receive the proper nutrients. However, to get a plant to produce 'usable' weed, you need to be sure you have invested in the project. It would not make sense to purchase low-quality stock and waste your time!

When procuring the seeds, be sure you have thoroughly researched the strain. Not all of the cannabis strains are capable of surviving outdoors. Check the reviews carefully and seek a reputable source for your supply of seeds.

Remember, it takes an expert a period of several years of breeding to provide quality seeds. The grower has to be sure the strain will remain stabilized when placed outside.

These are a few of the 'top picks' of 2016:

- **AK-47, 48, & 9 Seeds**

You will become mellow and relaxed with the Sativa-dominant hybrid—AK-47. Its pungent 'skunky' aroma was created by Serious Seeds in 1992. The blend is of the Afghani, Mexican, Thai, and Colombian varieties.

The taste will be sweet and floral—with the earthy and sour scent. Outdoor plants usually finish the flowering time by the end of October. Professional growers believe that it is easier to grow indoors with a hydroponic setup or soil, especially with a flowering time of only 53 to 63 days.

AK-47 can take the cold weather; but at the same time, it can stunt/slow down the plant's growth. It is excellent for outdoor gardens.

AK-48 shares the same high yields and fast cycle as the AK-47; but, it is smaller and produces more successfully in a warmer climate. It also has a strong aroma.

AK-9 is available and gaining popularity as an auto-flowering strain. It is also 'stinky' and likes the outdoors with extra space to grow. Hold onto your hat, with the euphoria; you will experience with a 'toke' of this one.

The THC level for this strain is at a minimum of 20% with a flowering time of 8 to 9 weeks. The plant is easy to grow and has received awards with High Times Cup Awards in 1999 and 2003— coming in at 2nd place both years.

- **Sensi Seeds—Guerrilla's Gusto**

With a bit of a pun is intended for this specific strain of cannabis, it has been said by the professionals that it 'grows like a weed.' This particular plant is best because it is pest and mold resistant and is typed as Indica dominant. The plant is so hardy that you can literally throw the seeds and return later when it's time for the harvest. Of course, you realize the seeds won't provide you with the same high yields, as if the light is right and water is supplied.

However, this isn't a feminized strain, so a 'sexing' site is essential to eliminate the possibility of buds full of seeds. If you are a beginner, you are asking what is sexing. The short answer is after the plant has about four to five weeks of growth, you will be able to tell whether you have a male or female plant.

You need to remove any male plants before they have the opportunity to fertilize/pollinate the females. If you don't move them, seeds will develop, and the THC will be diverted to the seeds (which is not cool at all). Simply stated, the females produce seeds and the males the pollen. Does it sound familiar?

This plant will provide medium THC levels with a seven to nine-week flowering time. As stated earlier, Sensi is simple to grow, making it an excellent choice for a beginner.

- **Vision—Northern Lights Auto-Flowering Fem**

This gal is a charm for a beginner because it needs minimal effort regarding fertilizer and can also handle various lighting effortlessly. The auto-flowering version will be 'weed' to smoke within eight weeks. You will discover that it is an excellent choice for medical users because of its deep relaxing and full-body power.

Many growers prefer the Northern Lights Auto over the original version because of its simplicity of growing ability to grow in varied climates and little feeding. These plants are smaller than the Northern Lights which can grow up to five to six feet tall. The original seeds also need a warm environment for survival.

The type is Indica/Ruderalis which will grow to the height of 100 cm to 130 cm (approximately three to four feet) with a yield of 30 grams to 50 grams per plant. It is also easily feminized with a 20% level of THC.

- **Lowryder—Lowryder 2 Auto-Feminized Seeds**

Lowryder 2 is excellent for those who do not have much available space because it grows low to the ground and only reaches approximately thirty inches. Its mild aroma adds to its appeal for growing in a window box or just hiding among the flowers. However, this Indica/Ruderalis/Sativa type one might not produce as much as some of the other outdoor strains; but, it will grow in the windows. Lowryder 2 has a low-medium THC level.

- **Dutch Passion—Holland's Hope Feminized Seeds**

If you live in a wet climate, this gal is the one for you; since, it is bred to be reliable in an unstable environment such as the United Kingdom, Canada, or the United States. This is a fabulous choice for short-season areas because you can see a harvest as quickly as fifty days from planting time.

The plant is a pest, fungus, and mold resistant and will produce a mild odor and a high yield. If you are searching for kick, you will get it with this Indica/Sativa knockout; so be prepared for a nap. Medical users boast of its use for chronic pain and depression. It can produce a 10% to 15% THC level with a flowering time of seven to nine weeks and will grow to medium height. This is also an excellent choice for a beginner.

- **Barney's Blue Cheese Auto Feminized**

This robust, stocky, short, Indica type plant is excellent for limited spaces, and usually only reaches a height of 80 cm (under three feet). Also, have no fear—the resin laden buds are the rewards for your hard work. Be careful with the pH balance because the strain is known for its susceptible imbalances of pH.

The seeds are vigorous from day one, providing you with a harvest within ten weeks after germination. Some of the other 'Cheese' varieties may produce more quantity, but this short gal will provide the quality. With the super high in CBD and the tasty smoke, it is a perfect 'laid-back' choice. Expect THC levels of 12% to 15%.

- **Ace—Bangi Haze Feminized Seeds**

This is a fabulous Sativa type of marijuana that is well-known for its pest and mold-resistant qualities. The plant was initially bred in Northern Spain, but can also thrive in damp/chilly northern areas. This Haze variety is one of the few capable of being harvested outdoors. It creates a Sativa/bubble possessing high THC levels. Within nine to ten weeks, the seedling will be flowering.

- **Barney's Farm: Barney's LSD Fem Seeds**

This jewel is hardy as a 'trippy' stone, as well as disease resistant qualities. If your choice is Indica;

you will be ready for this one. The plant will thrive easily in the woods or a field. Once again, it is easy to grow with a 20%+ THC level.

The list goes on, but these are just the top ones for the year that are excellent for outdoors and easier to harvest.

Germinate the Seeds

After you have your seeds, know the location, have the soil ready, and are prepared for some work, it's time to germinate your cannabis seeds. The germination methods mentioned are used for getting a head start on your crop inside. The first root is known as the 'taproot,' and is the first sign that you are ready to begin your planting.

The taproot—or maybe a few offshoots—will get longer and push the seed up. After the shell breaks the surface of the growing medium previously selected, the first cotyledons (round leaves) will appear inside the cannabis seed, which was already created in the seed itself as part of the plant embryo.

The next set, after the cotyledons, will have serrations/jagged edges that are called the first "true" leaves.

Essentials for Germination of the Seeds

For the best results you need to consider each of these elements:

- **Give the Seeds Peace**: Avoid messing with the seeds while the taproot matures.
- **Moisture for the Seeds**: Don't over-soak is the primary concern during germination. You should soak the hard seeds from twenty-four to thirty-two hours—no longer.
- **Keep the Seedlings Warm**: To get the best rates from germination, provide warmth—not hot. Think of springtime temperatures because germination may take longer under cooler conditions.

- **Be Gentle**: If you must move the seedlings, avoid touching the white root because it will be quickly snapped off in its fragile state.

- **Planting the Seeds**: For quality reasons, be sure the white root is downwards towards the growing medium to eliminate the plant from the task of reorienting for growth.

- **Plant the Seedlings Knuckle-Deep**: Consider the depth of planting the germinated seeds from 1.3 cm to 2.4 cm or about 1/2 inch to one-inch. As a guideline, they only need to be just under the growing medium.

Methods of Germination

Method 1

Seedling plugs and starter cubes are most recommended by professional growers. All this is necessary for placing the seed into the plug/cube and water as the manufacturer indicates making the seeds in gear under perfect germination conditions.

Rapid Rooters are appropriate and easy to work with, and the roots and sprouts should appear within several days. You can use them for any setup (in or out) and are manufactured by General Hydroponics (the same business used by NASA) for a consistent and quality product. You merely open the package and go. However, you can only purchase 50+ at a time—no less. If not used within one or two weeks, they will dry out.

Jiffy Pellets come highly recommended for soil or coco coir and are excellent for cloning. The significant advantage is the pellet form will last for a much longer time. You also must soak each of the pellets in warm water for expansion before use. After the pellet expands, gently squeeze out the excess amount of water, and you are ready to proceed with the seeds. They are not suited for hydroponic setups.

Method 2

Use a germination station with a heat mat, or you can make one by placing a plastic dome over a plate on a heating pad. A starter seedling cube will be used which makes transferring the seedling to the next medium or container easy. Rapid Growers also have an excellent starter cube that can be used with coco coir, hydroponics, or soil.

Method 3

Soaking the seeds overnight in slightly warm water will wake up the older seeds (more than several years old) or for seeds with tough shells. Most of the viable seeds will begin floating on top of the water and after several hours will sink to the bottom. You will be able to observe the first tap root breaking through the shell if you have the seeds in a clear glass.

Note: Don't become discouraged because some seeds may take longer than others, but never leave them in the water for more than twenty-four to thirty-two hours (previously mentioned, but it's essential). If after that time, you observe no growth, place the seeds in a moist, warm place to finish the germination process.

Method 4

The paper plate method is just placing the seeds in a wet paper towel and setting it in a warm area. This is not the best method because you could damage the tap root when moving the sprouts. Some growers recommend putting the towel and seeds between two paper plates or a dish turned upside down for germination.

Be sure to check on the seeds approximately every twelve hours and plant any seeds that have sprouted immediately.

How to Plant the Seeds

Use tweezers or use extreme caution, so you don't damage the root; that will be money down the drain if the taproot breaks. The plant has a slim chance of survival; but, its growth might be stunted from the start.

As mentioned earlier, roots down, knuckle deep, with the seed's top just below the growing medium's surface. You may see results from a few hours to a couple of days. However, if you haven't seen it break through after ten days, it may not survive if the root was unsuitably placed. Sometimes you lose a few seeds—it's normal.

You are ahead of the game and ready to take them outside if you started inside early. You also don't have to be concerned about the inclement weather which could damage the seedlings. You can use a constant LED light until early springtime which gives you the correct lighting for your baby seedlings. However, you must consider that they are pricey. If you are into production for the long haul, they could be a worthy investment.

Chapter 5: Harvesting and Drying Techniques

Before you begin the harvest, you must make sure you must let the flowering stage start.

The Vegetative & Flowering Cycle

The flowering stage begins with the late summer lengthening nights occur. Some species may stop the vegetative production promptly, while others could quadruple in size. The span of 55 to 70 days for buds to mature after the plants begin the flowering process is a general 'rule of thumb.' As it begins, be sure to switch flowering to a 'bloom' mixture, so the essential nutrients will produce larger buds.

Week One–Two: Conversion to Flowering

This stage is considered the first stage of life for a marijuana plant. The plant literally grows like a weed. The plant can grow several inches in one day with its new stems and leaves.

During the second week of the flowering process, small buds will appear. You will also see what seem to be white hairs called pistols sprouting from the plant. That proves you have a female plant. Continue feeding the nutrients as previously mentioned for the plant to provide its maximum yield. With the particular nutrients, your bud quality should remain in excellent condition without any deficiencies until harvest time.

As the days begin to shorten, the plants will make buds in late summer; but as previously mentioned, it would depend on the local climate factors as well. The uninterrupted dark periods push the plant to flower when the dark time exceeds the critical time period which varies between eight to eleven hours. The higher latitudes will benefit plants with a short dark period.

Week Three: Bud Formation

At this point, the plant should be approximately 25% to 50% larger than when you began the flowering process. A few trichomes and resin glands are present during this week which is a glimpse of what the plant will become. The aroma is not offensive at this point (if you call the smell bad).

Week Four–Five: Buds Begin to Get Fat

During week four, the vegetative stage is complete, and the plant will begin to focus all energy on the flowering phase. Massive changes will occur as the buds start to show 'themselves' at various bud sites. In week four, as the plant produces capitate trichomes, the odor will be more evident.

Week five presents a sharp increase for bud production with the thicker existing bud sites as new sites appear along the first section.

Week Six–Eight: Pistils Darken, Buds Ripen

At this time, the plant won't make any newer stems and leaves. It has changed gears (away from vegetative growth) and is ready to focus on growing the bud from now until its harvest time. You may notice that some of the bottom leaves are yellowing; but, this is normal. However, it indicates that it has a light burn or nutrient issue. You must react fast, so you don't hurt your yields.

Watch closely for 'spire' or whole new buds emerging from the side of an already developed bud. This is possibly caused by light damage or too much heat. This environment will cause 'fox-tailing,' as well as burn/discolor/bleach your buds. The heat or excessive light may also cause some of the THCs' potency to evaporate.

Week Eight: The Flowering Cycle Ends

The flowers are ripe by the end of the week with the peak zone in the last seventy-two hours. After that stage, you must harvest, or they will begin to deteriorate.

How to Trigger the Flowering Stage

If you get tired of growing the plants and want to trigger the plants into the flowering stage, you can by covering the plants daily during the summer to trigger to the plant that it is 'nighttime.'

For example, you could cover the plants at 9:00 p.m. and uncover them at 9:00 a.m. by using an opaque cover over the garden during that time.

Top Tie Down

At this point, you can choose to bind down or top the cannabis plants if you have limited space. By trimming the plant, you will have two main tops instead of the original one. They will yield more but won't grow as tall. You can pull the most prominent bud down and bind it with a bit of tension, which will provide the same effect as topping it off, but the most prominent bud is retained. The final result will be larger buds, and the lower branches will have better growth.

Support the Plant

You might need to support the limbs of the marijuana plant with a trellis, plant stakes, or tomato cages. If left alone (no topping or pruning), the plant will grow in the shape of a Christmas tree which would not need any additional support. However, when you top them, you are doubling the shoots with each clip.

You will create a hormonal change when you cut the top-most part of the pot plant. This first step will result in the plants forming bushes rather than becoming tall.

You can place trellis netting to the appropriate level, so your tops will grow through the netting. It might take more than one net. The mesh will prevent some of the breakages of the stalks while producing longer/thicker and larger marijuana plants.

Trichome and Bud Development

Since the flowering stages differ significantly among strains—beginning and progressing at different rates and different maturing times—it's essential to closely watch the plants to know where they are in the development phase. Two indicators are evident—which is the pistil color and the appearance of the trichome.

If you have an immature 'pot' flower, the trichomes are clear, whereas the hair-like pistils have a white appearance. When mature, the pistils will become orange or red and turn inward as the flowers begin to mature.

You will probably need a magnifying glass to see the trichomes coloring bit the pistil color is easily observed. The professional growers suggest that the magnification should be between 40-× and

100-× to clearly see the progress from clear to milky and amber in color.

When 40% of the pistils have darkened, on the early side, and half of the trichomes have turned clear to milky, you will receive a more dynamic buzz/high effect since the THC hasn't yet had time to degrade into CBN. The CBN is what provides the stoner-couch effect.

If you wait until the trichomes are milky or 50 to 70% of the pistils have darkened, you will receive a more intense buzz because the THC is the most highly concentrated in the cloudy trichomes.

If you allow some of the pistils to become 70 to 90% darkened and the trichomes turn amber, more THC is transformed into CBN which will make the plant more suitable for treating insomnia and anxiety.

Chapter 6: Extract Preparation

Flushing the Plants

You have to be sure you have all of the essential equipment before you begin your harvest. You will need to have your trimming and drying spaces ready, along with a good pair of trimming scissors. You can also flush out the nutrients from the soil before the time you are ready for harvesting so that the plant will use up its food reserves. You want all of the starches and sugars to be removed which will produce a harsher smoke.

The process should begin ideally two weeks before harvest time. The process involved is not a long one but is essential.

- **Step 1**: Use a large quantity of water and flood the containers to remove the built-up nutrients. For a few minutes, let them rest.

- **Step 2**: Once again, flood the soil to remove the nutrients.
- **Step 3**: Several days later, you will notice the leaves have begun to yellow, which indicates a nitrogen deficiency. This is normal, so the plant will focus its energy on bud development, and lose a few of the lower/larger leaves. This will create a surge of energy for the rest of the plant.

When the Crop is Ready

You have followed all of the rules from the seeds, germination, flowering, budding—the whole works. You have to know a few tricks to be sure your timing is perfect.

How You Know for Sure the Crop is Ready

Once the plant begins to lose its vibrant green color, it is an excellent idea to pick them. If they are brown, the weed will be harsher to smoke. The leaves and buds will change quickly, indicating the plant is dying. On the flip side, there will be more resin in the resin glands to achieve a stronger, more intense buzz.

As you gain experience, it will be much easier to tell if you harvested too soon or too late. It is all normal.

Tips of How to Harvest the Crop

You are at the finish line now! Follow these procedures for a perfect crop:

- **Be Sure You Beat the Frost in Your Area**. Try choosing a beautiful crisp day with plenty of sun and clear skies. If it rains, it will just increase drying time slightly. It will not have an effect on the resin glands or the buds. Stay alert, and you should be safe as long as you have a friend to follow close behind if you are placing the 'weed' in your vehicle. Incognito is the word-of-the-day!

- **Bring the Bags**: It is essential to bring some large bags for the harvest; but, if you bring the transparent ones, be sure to bring along some black ones for safety purposes. Cut the plants in easily transported lengths to easily fit into your bags. It is important not to spend a lot of time on-location. You must be efficient and fast.
- **Wear Disposable Gloves**: It is recommended using gloves to prevent the sticky resin from sticking to your hands as you are trimming the plant.

Dry & Cure the Crop

The job is not quite over until the buds go through the curing process, which involves using a controlled environment with the buds in glass jars so specific plant processes will occur. Cure them right every time with these items:

- **Wide-mouth Mason Jars**: You can purchase these in many locations such as a large grocery store or a superstore like Wal-Mart. It is ideal to use the one-quart size which will hold approximately 0.75 to 1.25 ounces of marijuana (depending on its consistency).

- **A Place to Dry the Weed**: Many of the professionals will hang the buds from clothes hangers in a closet, but you can use almost anything with a bit of string. Some use a drying rack (optional), but it is generally used only if you have a lot of buds to be dried in a small area or if there is an issue of high humidity. During normal/average humidity conditions, the racks can dry out the buds too fast.

- **Humidipaks**: (Optional) These packs are reasonable and explicitly formulated for storing cannabis to prevent it from getting crispy or dry. The Boveda Medium 62%

packs are recommended and are found on Amazon.

- **Hygrometer**: (Optional) If you choose to use a hygrometer to measure the humidity inside the jar, the Caliber IV Hygrometer (for sale on Amazon) will easily fit inside. You want to be sure it isn't too dry or humid to provide optimal curing.

Step One: Cut the Plant Down

Each grower has his/her way of cutting the plant. Some will cut the branches from the mother plant and hang them up to dry; while others will trim the plant at the base and hang the entire plant. Whereas, others choose to cut off the individual buds and lay them on a rack or mesh screen to dry. You can lay them out on cardboard or by placing them in paper bags. This phase is the grower's choice.

Step Two: Trim Extra Fan Leaves

Most growers will trim away any extra leaves, mainly the big fan leaves, but some also trim the smaller ones that grow on the buds. Too much leafy material will make the 'pot' harsh, and the trim job will provide a smoother/improved appearance of the buds. Once again, it's up to you. However, you need to consider if your area is very humid; you want to remove as much as you can to prevent mold and speed up the drying process.

These are some of the humidity factors to consider:

- **Average Humidity Levels**: You have the perfect location to hang the cannabis upside down to dry if you don't experience high humidity factors in your area.
- **Humidity Over 60%**: The buds should probably be separated from the branches after they are trimmed. It is advisable to use

mesh or a drying rack to prevent the mold
issues.

- **Dry—Under 30% Relative Humidity**:
More leaves should be left on the plant
during the trimming process to slow down
the drying process. Try leaving some of the
fan leaves or not trim until after the buds
are dried.

Tip: Save the trimmed leaves. You can use them
later to make some marijuana butter or similar
cannabis extracts. If you have the time, you will be
surprised how many things you can make with
them. (The items could fill another book.)

Step Three: The Slow Drying Process Begins

For the best curing environment, you should have
50% humidity with the room around 70°F/21°C.
These are some of the ways you can adjust the
chosen space:

- **Evaporative Cooler**: Raises the humidity and cools the air
- **Dehumidifier**: Lowers humidity and heats the air
- **Humidifier**: Raises the humidity
- **Air Conditioner**: Lowers the humidity and cools the air
- **Heater**: Heats the air

Tip: Avoid using a dehydrator/stove, a microwave, or dry ice because the buds will smell and taste dreadful, and may also leave you paranoid or with a migraine. This will skip the most essential stage of the curing process. Even mildly hot temperatures (for example 85°F/30°C) can burn off some of the cannabinoids and terpenes (valuable smells).

Approximately 50% of the bud quality depends on the curing stage. You can leave as much of the stem as you wish; but, it will slow the drying process if you leave a more substantial portion on the plant. Use the method of your choice, and consider using a closet or grow tent to dry the newly harvested buds.

As a word of caution, if you use a section of cardboard for drying, it is essential to rotate the buds after several hours for more even drying. You will also have imprints on the sides of the bud where they touched a flat surface during the drying phase. It does work well if you are in an extremely humid climate.

Try using a fan to create extra air flow, but never directly on the buds. Aim the air towards a close wall. The fan can cause them to dry too quickly and cause them to over-dry. Slow-drying is essential; meaning you should check the buds daily until you understand how to dry them in your space.

Step Four: Continue Drying

The process of drying should continue until the smaller stems snap, not bend. The outside of the bud should be dry to the touch, approximately three to seven days. If they dry before three or four days, you have allowed the buds to dry too quickly. This will slow the curing process and almost stop it. But, they will cure; it will just take a bit longer.

If you removed the stems, it is vital to place the buds into the jar as soon as the buds are dry to the touch. Some growers are tempted to sample the product at this point, but it will tend to give you a headache and throat issues because it's too harsh. Besides, it needs to be cured to reach optimal potency.

Step Five: Put the Buds into Jars

At this stage, the humidity levels in the jars should be 60 to 65% with the room temperature approximately 70°F/21°C (same as step 3). You will want to leave some 'breathing' room, so only use 75% of each jar. When you shake the jar, the buds need to move around. You might need to remove the lid for a short time if they are sticking together. The process in jars is approximately two or months.

Tip: If you smell ammonia, they are too wet and bad bacteria is beginning to grow.

Step Six: Open Jars and Inspect

As previously stated, you will want to check the buds daily to ensure you don't have any bacterial growth. This process should continue for the first few weeks during the curing process to 'air out' the buds.

Chapter 7: Easy Cannabis Recipes

You will be surprised how easy it is to prepare so many items using cannabis; but first, let's have a cup of tea.

All you need to do to enjoy a cup of tea is prepare it as usual and add 1 teaspoon of cannabis butter. Sweeten it up with a splash of milk and portion of honey.

Sit back and enjoy.

These are a few items to have for preparation in baking:

- A grinder
- A mixing bowl
- A cake oven tin
- Non-stick spray or lining paper
- An oven
- A microwave

- A skewer
- Optional: A wire rack

High Potency Cannabis Butter

What You Need:

- Weed—preferably with 15% THC, 7–10 grams
- Butter—1 pound, 4 sticks
- Water—4 cups

How to Prepare:

1. Decarb Your Cannabis. Bake your lightly ground cannabis flowers for 30 minutes at 250°F (120°C).
2. Boil the water in a semi-deep cooking pot. Add the butter and wait for it to melt, all the while stirring and mixing the pot.
3. Add the decarbed cannabis to the mixture. Lower the temperature and simmer—don't boil—the mixture for 20–30 minutes.
4. Strain the mixture through cheesecloth into a glass bowl or a jar. Leave it on top of the cheesecloth to strain thoroughly. The bulk

of the plant material should be in the cheesecloth.

5. Store in the fridge for 5–6 hours. The butter will form a crust on top and separate from the water.

6. Cut the butter out. Use a knife to cut it out and then you can re-melt it in your microwave or just use it in a recipe.

Canna-butter Dosing

Keeping that in mind, and the fact that edibles are always a bit stronger than smoking, here's what is considered standard dosing for edibles:

- *First Timers*: 5–10 mg of THC
- *Light Users*: 20–30 mg of THC
- *Casual Users*: 50–70 mg of THC
- *Heavy Users*: (+) 100 mg of THC

Weed Brownies in Style

What You Need:

- Cannabis bud/the equivalent strength in cuttings—8 grams
- Flour—1.75 cups
- Non-salted butter—1 cup
- Granulated sugar—1 cup
- Milk—.75 cup
- Eggs—2
- Baking powder—1.75 tsp.
- Salt—.5 tsp.
- Any other ingredients you want to improve the cake with, such as cocoa powder, vanilla extract, dried fruit, icing/frosting, buttercream, chocolate chips, or anything else—your imagination is your only limit.

How to Prepare:

1. Grind up all your cannabis until it's a fine consistency.
2. Warm up the oven to 374°F or 190°C.

3. Toss the butter in a bowl and place it in the microwave for 20 seconds until it's a pasty consistency. Combine the cannabis with the butter.

4. Mix the flour, all of the sugar, canna-butter, milk, cannabis butter, eggs, plus anything else you want to your mixing bowl. Mix well for several minutes; but, it will ensure your cannabis is spread evenly as possible throughout the cake mix. Note: Add a splash of milk if the mix is a little bit too dry; if it is too wet, just add some extra flour.

5. Grease the cake tin with non-stick spray, or line a layer of non-stick parchment paper.

6. Pour the batter into the tin, spreading it around so that it is evenly distributed. Bake in the preheated oven for 25 minutes.

7. After 25 minutes, test the center of the cake with a skewer. If it comes out clean, it is ready; if it sticks to the skewer, let it bake for about five more minutes.

8. Let the cake to cool for about 20 minutes in the tin. Then, place it upside down on the wire rack and remove the tin. Let the cake continue to cool for an additional 30 minutes.

9. Once cooled, decorate the cake with anything you want, serve and enjoy!

Chocolate-Covered Strawberries

What You Need:

- Dark chocolate chips—1 cup
- Canna-butter—2 tbsp.
- Fresh strawberries
- For the Garnish: Flaky sea salt

How to Prepare:

1. Heat up a double boiler or use the microwave to melt the canna-butter and chips.
2. When the mixture is creamy smooth, just dip the berries and place on a parchment paper-lined tin.
3. Drizzle with the sea salt and let them cool at room temperature or in the fridge.

5-Minute Chocolate Mug Cake

What You Need:

- Cocoa powder—2 tbsp.
- Flour—4 tbsp.
- Sugar—4 tbsp.
- Chocolate chips—1 handful
- Egg—1
- Also Needed: Large microwave safe drinking mug

How to Prepare:

1. Mix everything up and add in anything else you may want, such as berries, marshmallows or vanilla extract.
2. Next, mix in some cannabis butter—however much you want (go by the chart).
3. Put in the microwave and cook for 3–5 minutes, and it will be ready to enjoy!

The Fire Cracker

What You Need for 1 Serving:

- Peanut butter—1–2 tbsp.
- Graham cracker sheet—1
- Weed—1 gram

How to Prepare:

1. Warm up the oven to 325°F or 160 °C. Layer a baking tin with a sheet of foil.
2. Break the cracker into half and spread the peanut butter on half.
3. Grind the weed to a fine substance and sprinkle over the top. Once the pieces are joined the oil in the peanut butter will extract the THC.
4. Close each cracker and wrap in the foil. Make as many as you like.
5. Bake for 25 to 30 minutes. Add a drizzle of honey or some agave syrup to top it off.

Asian Pear Cannabis Gazpacho

What You Need for 1 Serving:

- Cherry tomatoes—1 cup
- Asian pear—.5 of 1
- Garlic cloves—2
- Minced ginger—2 tsp.
- Roughly chopped green onions—2
- Seeded jalapeno—1
- Fresh cannabis juice—3 tbsp. or 1 canna-cube**
- Toasted sesame oil—.5 tsp.
- Fish sauce—1 tbsp.
- Apple cider vinegar—1 tbsp.
- To taste: White pepper & salt
- Optional—1 sliced toasted bread
- Optional—1 pinch sesame seeds

How to Prepare:

1. In a blender, combine each of the fixings:
   The tomatoes, pear, garlic, jalapeno, onions,

juice of cannabis, oil, and vinegar. Puree until creamy smooth.

2. Sprinkle with salt and pepper to your liking.

3. Top it off with a few halved cherry tomatoes, shredded scallions, and sesame seeds. Toast a slice of bread and enjoy!

**Canna Cubes

1. All you need is some fresh cannabis juice.

2. Pour the juice into ice cube trays approximately 2/3 of the way to full.

3. Lightly cover the tray with a plastic and freeze. Once frozen solid pop them out and store in freezer bags.

Winter Spice Banana Paleo Pancakes

What You Need for the Batter:

- Mashed bananas—2
- Eggs—2
- Cinnamon—0.125 tsp. or 1 pinch
- Oil spray

What You Need for the Topping:

- Paleo Maple Syrup—2 tbsp.
- Cannabis-infused Ghee—equaling 20 mg or 2 tbsp.
- Each one: Ginger, clove, cardamom, and cinnamon—1 pinch or .0125 tsp

How to Prepare:

1. Heat up a pan using medium heat on the stovetop.
2. Combine the egg, banana, and cinnamon. Whisk them with a fork until combined. (It may be lumpy.)

3. Once your pan is hot, spritz it with a layer of cooking oil spray.

4. Pour pancake batter in 2–3 tablespoons at a time. Once bubbles start to form on top you can flip. (At this point, you can add the CBD chocolate chunks or pecans.)

5. The banana will caramelize and smell amazing. Once both sides are cooked, remove from the pan and top with your warm cannabis-infused Winter Spice Ghee Syrup.

6. Serve and enjoy the four pancakes!

Cannabis-Infused Waffles

What You Need:

- Eggs—2
- Salt—.5 tsp.
- Vanilla extract—1 tsp.
- Baking powder—4 tsp.
- Granulated sugar—1 tbsp.
- Self-rising flour—2 cups
- Warm milk—2 cups
- Canna-butter—.5 cup

How to Prepare:

1. Warm up the waffle iron.
2. As it is warming, whisk the eggs until fluffy. Stir in the melted butter, milk, sugar, salt baking powder, vanilla extract, and flour.
3. Stir well until the mixture is creamy.
4. Spritz the heated waffle iron with some cooking oil spray. Add the mixture, cook, and enjoy.

'Baked' Potato

What You Need:

- Russet potato—cleaned—1
- Canna-butter—1 tbsp.
- Sour cream 2 tbsp. (+) more for garnish
- Cheddar cheese—grated—.25 cup
- Salt and pepper—to your liking
- For the garnish: Crispy bacon & chives

How to Prepare:

1. Warm up the oven to reach 400°F or 200 °C. Arrange the potato on the oven rack or cookie tin and bake for 45 minutes to 1 hour.
2. Transfer to the countertop to cool for handling.
3. Use a sharp knife to open the skin (make an x). Remove the flesh and add the fixings together (not the garnishes). Add the filling back into the skin and replace the top.

4. When it's all bubbly (about 10 min.), just remove and top as you like it. Enjoy!

Maca-stoni & Cheese

- Cooked macaroni noodles—.5 lb.
- Canna-butter—4 tbsp.
- All-purpose flour—4 tbsp.
- Whole milk, warmed—3
- Sharp cheddar cheese, grated—4 oz.
- Smoked Gouda cheese, grated—4 oz.
- Gruyere cheese, grated—4 oz.
- Smoked paprika—1 tsp.
- Garlic powder—1 tsp.
- Salt and pepper, to taste
- For the Garnish: FUNYUNS® & Chives

How to Prepare:

1. Cook the macaroni according to the package instructions.
2. Use a saucepan and combine the flour and canna-butter. Simmer using the med-low heat setting.
3. Whisk in the warmed milk, simmering until almost a boil (5 min.).

4. Combine the rest of the fixings (paprika, cheeses, salt, pepper, and garlic powder). When warmed and melted to make a sauce; fold in the cooked macaroni.

5. Serve the pasta in a serving dish and top it off with the FUNYUNS. Munch on!

Conclusion

You are now ready to start your crop, right?
Everyone makes a mistake, once in a while. These
are a few additional pointers so you can avoid
some of the pitfalls for first-time growers:

Making the initial investment in growing cannabis
is always helpful to take the advice of growers who
have already faced with the same issues you might
be facing with during your first growing
experience. These are just a few of the mistakes to
avoid:

- **Mistake 1: Overfeeding**: It is best to follow
  the directions provided by the manufacturer.
- **Mistake 2: Overwatering medium-based
  plants**: If you have decided to use
  buckets/pots for your plants; you will need to
  use a hefting approach. That is when you judge
  its weight by 'hefting.' First, you want to judge
  its dry weight—via hefting. Water the plant
  until the water is running through the drain

holes—heft again. When the pot feels the same wet as it did dry, it is time to water again. It is basically common sense.

- **Mistake 3: Over-Analyzing**: Watching the 'weed' grow is similar to watching a first born child. You don't want to miss a single thing. However, don't try to fix every yellow leaf you see; watch out for the big ones.

- **Mistake 4: Overspending on Materials**: If you are a beginner, try to stay on a set budget. It is easy to get 'caught up' in the excitement of it all. Just 'Buyer Beware.' Get down to the basics; but, get the good seeds such as the ones described in this book to have a high yielding crop.

You have all of the tools, so get started with your new project today!